"He that dwelleth in the secret place of the most High shall abide under the shadow of the Almighty"

(Psalm 91:1)

This Prayer and Fasting Journal Belongs To

My Prayer and Fasting Journal: Daily Moments of Prayer and
Fasting In The Secret Place

Introduction

Congratulations!   You have made a decision to embark on a time of prayer and fasting and this will indeed make a positive impact upon your life.

Your prayer and fasting journal is designed to assist you in building a stronger, more intimate relationship with God. In your journal you will find the following:

- **Prayer Scriptures** - Powerful Bible verses at the bottom of pages regarding prayer.
- **Fasting Scriptures** - Bible verses regarding persons who fasted such as Queen Esther and Daniel.
- **Bible prompts** - To guide you as you spend time in the Secret Place in prayer with your Heavenly Father.
- **Prayer Focus Topics** - A list of areas you may want to focus on such as prayers for your nation and family.
- **My Prayer** - Full pages to journal your praise and thanksgiving to God, prayer requests, and those areas which may be on your heart.
- **Answered Prayers** - A place you can track answered prayers.
- **Grocery List** - Prior to your fast, you can write those grocery items you wish to purchase in preparation for your fast.
- **Notes Pages** - Pages you can jot down notes in general.

Wherefore have we fasted, say they, and thou seest not? Wherefore have we afflicted our soul, and thou takest no knowledge? Behold, in the day of your fast ye find pleasure, and exact all your labours.

Behold, ye fast for strife and debate, and to smite with the fist of wickedness: ye shall not fast as ye do this day, to make your voice to be heard on high.

Is it such as fast that I have chosen? a day for a man to afflict his soul? Is it to bow down his head as a bulrush, and to spread sackcloth and ashes under him? Wilt though call this a fast, and an acceptable day to the LORD?

Is not this the fast that I have chosen? to loose the bands of wickedness, to undo the heavy burdens, and to let the oppressed go free, and that ye break every yoke?

Is it not the fast to deal thy bread to the hungry, and that thou bring the poor that are cast out to thy house? when though seest the naked, that thou cover him; and that thou hide not thyself from thine own flesh?

Isaiah 58:3-7

What is the purpose or goal for your time of prayer and fasting?

Date:______________________________

My Purpose for Embarking on This Time of Prayer and Fasting

1. Prayer of Adoration
2. Prayer of Praise and Thanksgiving
3. Prayer for Israel
4. Prayer for Religious Leaders
5. Prayer for Governmental Leaders and Other Persons in Authority
6. Prayer for your Nation and the Government
7. Prayer for the Continents of the World
8. Prayer for Missions
9. Prayer for Current Global Issues
10. Prayer for those who are Persecuted because of the Gospel
11. Prayer for the Hungry, Abused and Oppressed
12. Prayer for Revival
13. Prayer for your Family
14. Prayer for your Local Church
15. Prayer for the Global Church
16. Prayer for Forgiveness and Repentance
17. Prayer for Spiritual Insight, Wisdom, and your Walk with God
18. Prayer for your Physical Needs
19. Prayer for Deliverance from Evil

Let us begin!

Date: _______________________

My Key Verse for Today

____

____

____

____

Lord I thank You for

____

____

____

____

____

____

Today, I will pray for the following persons

____

____

____

____

____

____

My Reflections for Today

Lord I need Your divine assistance with this need

Lord I need help in my spiritual walk in this area

"He regards the prayer of the destitute and does not despise their prayer" (Psalm 102:17).

Date: _______________________

My Key Verse for Today

____

____

____

____

Lord I thank You for

____

____

____

____

____

____

Today, I will pray for the following persons

____

____

____

____

____

____

My Reflections for Today

Lord I need Your divine assistance with this need

Lord I need help in my spiritual walk in this area

"But when you pray, go into your room and shut the door and pray to your Father who is in secret. And your Father who sees in secret will reward you" (Matthew 6:6).

Esther's Fast

"Go, gather together all the Jews that are present in Shushan, and fast ye for me, and neither eat nor drink three days, night or day: I also and my maidens will fast likewise; and so will I go in unto the king, which is not according to the law: and if I perish, I perish." (Esther 4:16).

Date: _______________________

My Key Verse for Today

____

____

____

____

Lord I thank You for

____

____

____

____

____

____

Today, I will pray for the following persons

____

____

____

____

____

____

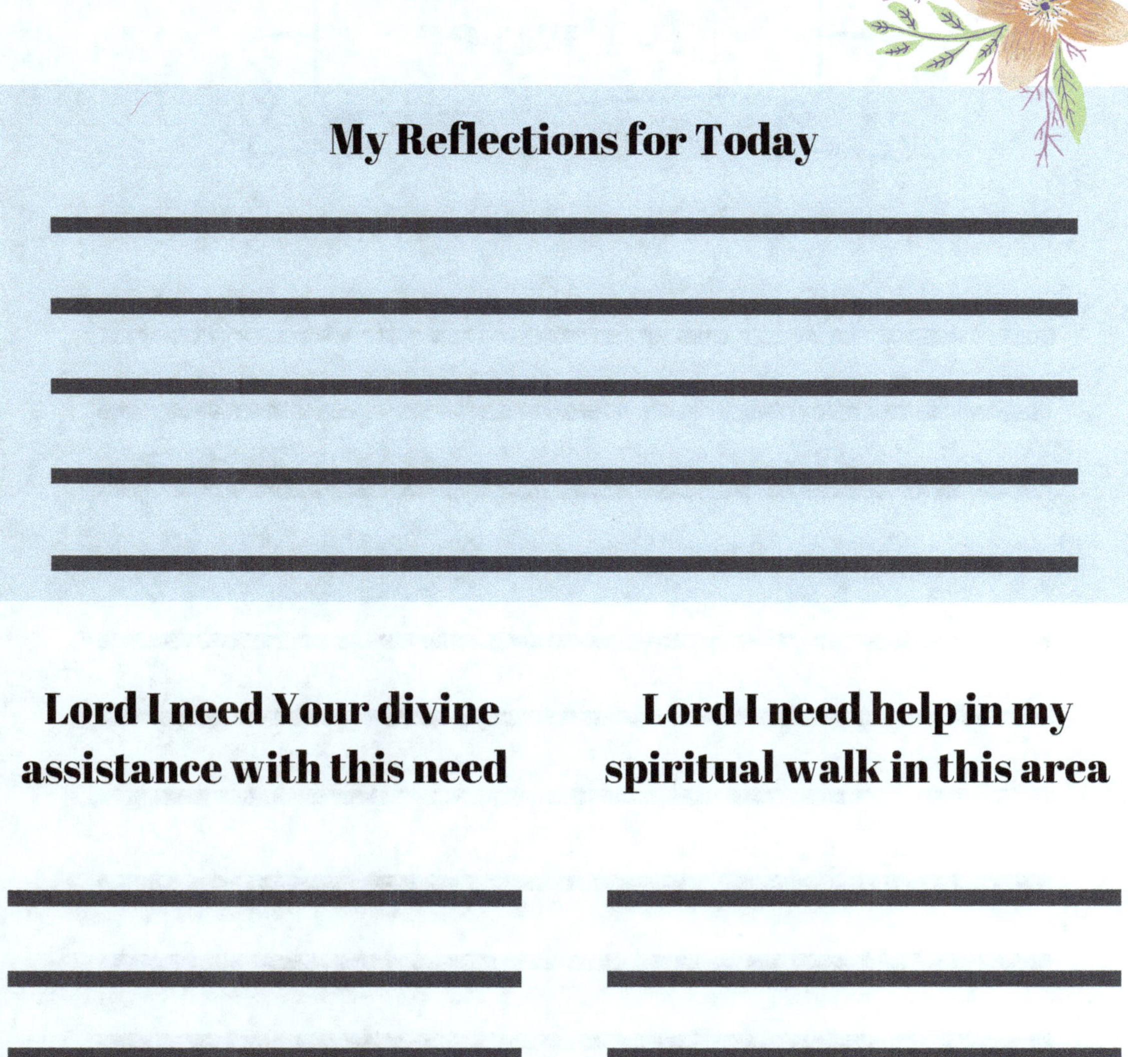

My Reflections for Today

Lord I need Your divine assistance with this need

Lord I need help in my spiritual walk in this area

____

____

____

____

____

____

____

____

____

____

"Watch and pray that you may not enter into temptation. The spirit indeed is willing, but the flesh is weak" (Matthew 26.41).

Date: ___________________________

My Key Verse for Today

____

____

____

____

Lord I thank You for

Today, I will pray for the following persons

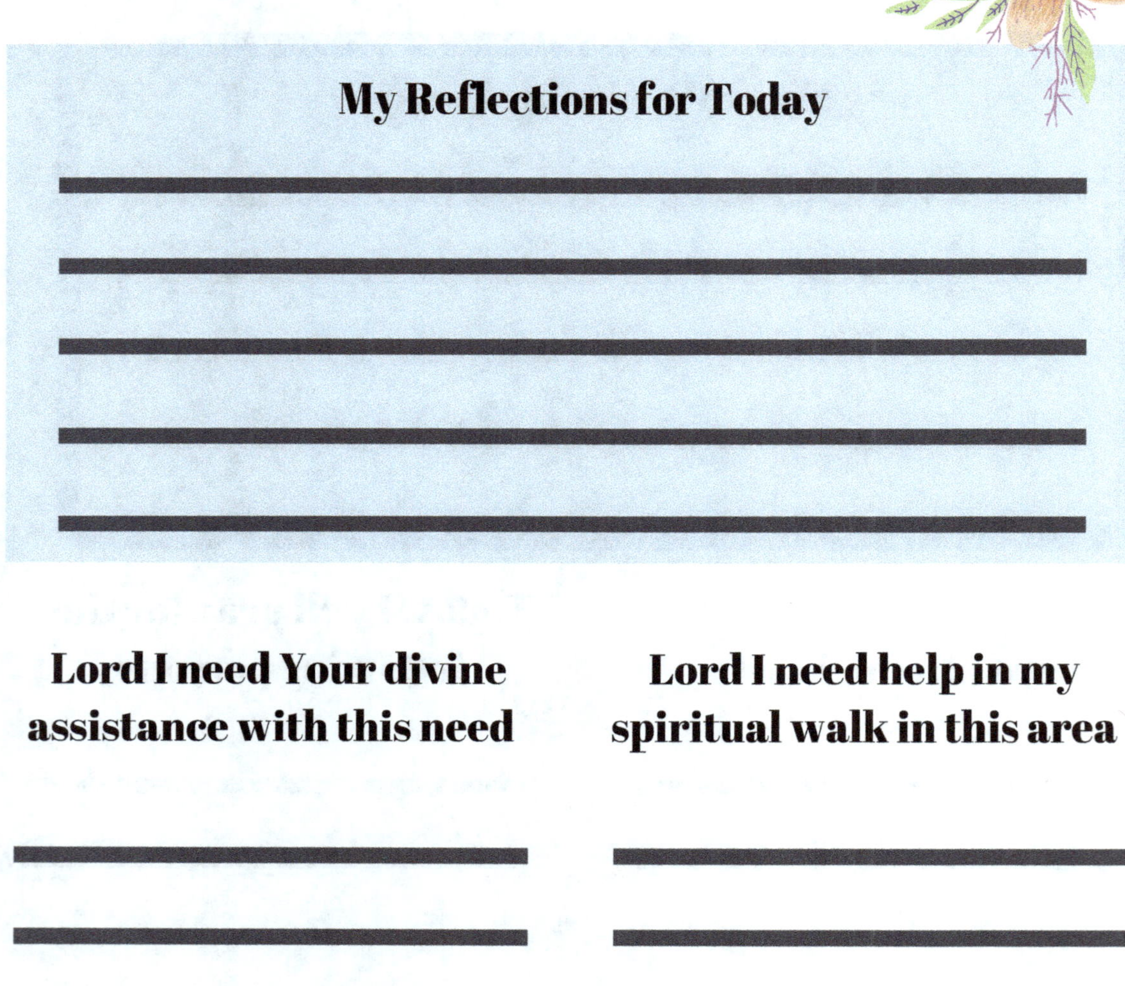

My Reflections for Today

Lord I need Your divine assistance with this need

Lord I need help in my spiritual walk in this area

"And whenever you stand praying, forgive, if you have anything against anyone, so that your Father also who is in heaven may forgive you your trespasses" (Mark 11:25).

Date:

My Key Verse for Today

Lord I thank You for

Today, I will pray for the following persons

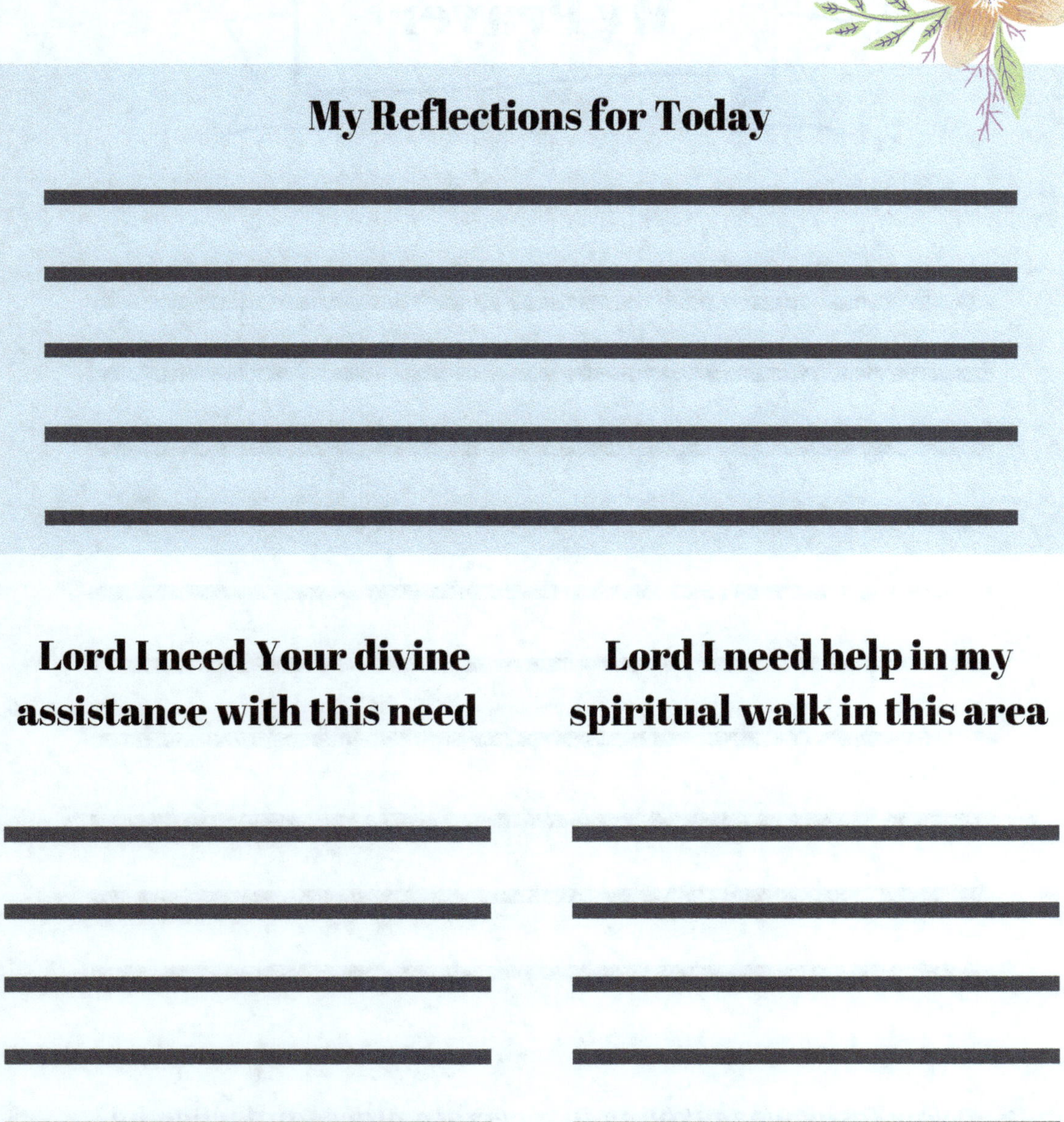

My Reflections for Today

Lord I need Your divine assistance with this need

Lord I need help in my spiritual walk in this area

My Prayer

"Now Jesus was praying in a certain place, and when he finished, one of his disciples said to him, "Lord, teach us to pray, as John taught his disciples." (Luke 11:1).

Daniel's Fast
(21 Days)

"Then said he unto me, Fear not, Daniel: for from the first day that thou didst set thine heart to understand, and to chasten thyself before thy God, thy words were heard, and I am come for thy words. (Daniel 10:14).

Date: _______________________

My Key Verse for Today

____

____

____

____

Lord I thank You for

____

____

____

____

____

____

Today, I will pray for the following persons

____

____

____

____

____

____

My Reflections for Today

Lord I need Your divine assistance with this need

Lord I need help in my spiritual walk in this area

"First of all, then, I urge that supplications, prayers, intercessions, and thanksgivings be made for all people," (1Timothy 2:1).

Date: ______________________________

My Key Verse for Today

Lord I thank You for

Today, I will pray for the following persons

My Reflections for Today

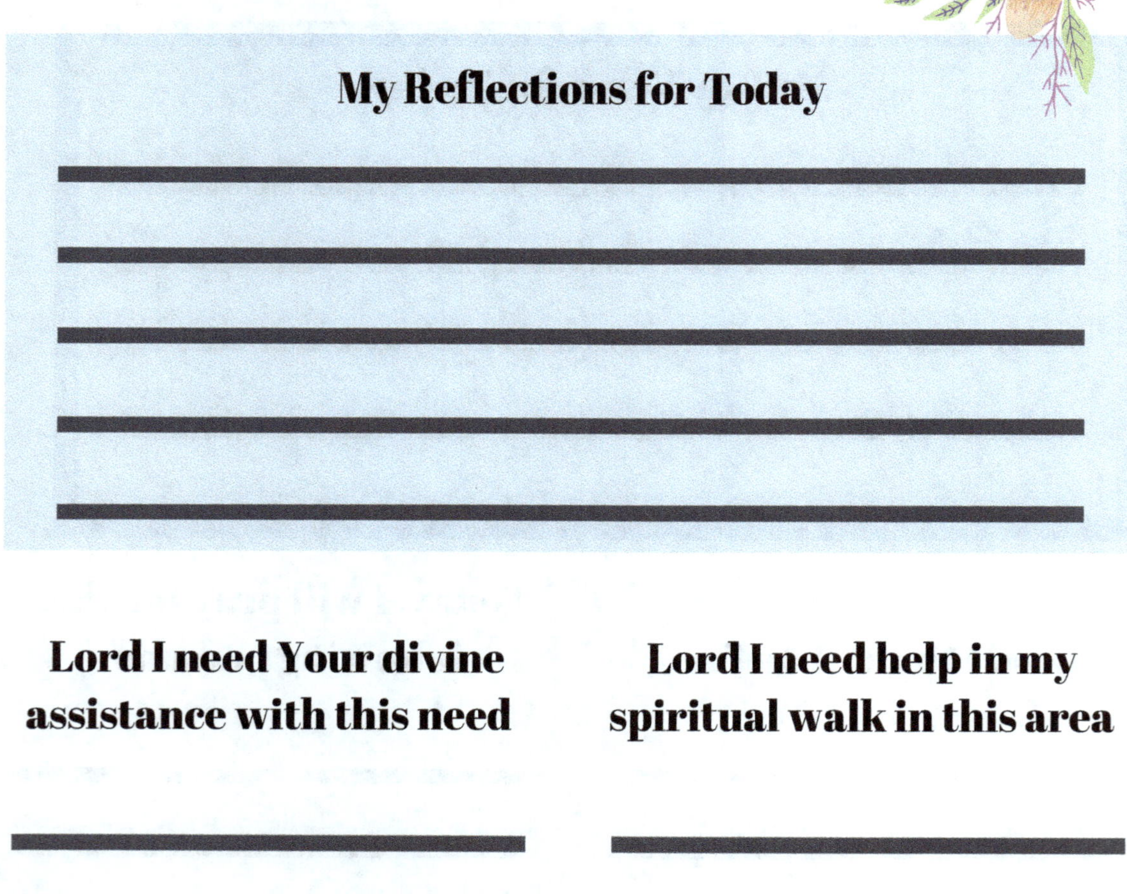

Lord I need Your divine assistance with this need

Lord I need help in my spiritual walk in this area

My Prayer

"Evening and morning and at noon I utter my complaint and moan, and he hears my voice" (Psalm 55:17)

Date: _______________________

My Key Verse for Today

____

____

____

____

Lord I thank You for

____

____

____

____

____

____

Today, I will pray for the following persons

____

____

____

____

____

____

My Reflections for Today

Lord I need Your divine assistance with this need

Lord I need help in my spiritual walk in this area

"Pray for the peace of Jerusalem! "May they be secure who love you!" (Psalm 122:6)

Samuel's Fast

"And they gathered together to Mizpeh, and drew water, and poured it out before the Lord, and fasted on that day, and said there, We have sinned against the Lord. And Samuel judged the children of Israel in Mizpeh" (1 Samuel 7:6)

Date: ______________________

My Key Verse for Today

____

____

____

____

Lord I thank You for

____

____

____

____

____

____

Today, I will pray for the following persons

____

____

____

____

____

____

My Reflections for Today

Lord I need Your divine assistance with this need

Lord I need help in my spiritual walk in this area

My Prayer

"Seek the Lord while he may be found; call upon him while he is near;" (Isaiah 55:6)

Date: _______________________

My Key Verse for Today

____

____

____

____

Lord I thank You for

____

____

____

____

____

____

Today, I will pray for the following persons

____

____

____

____

____

____

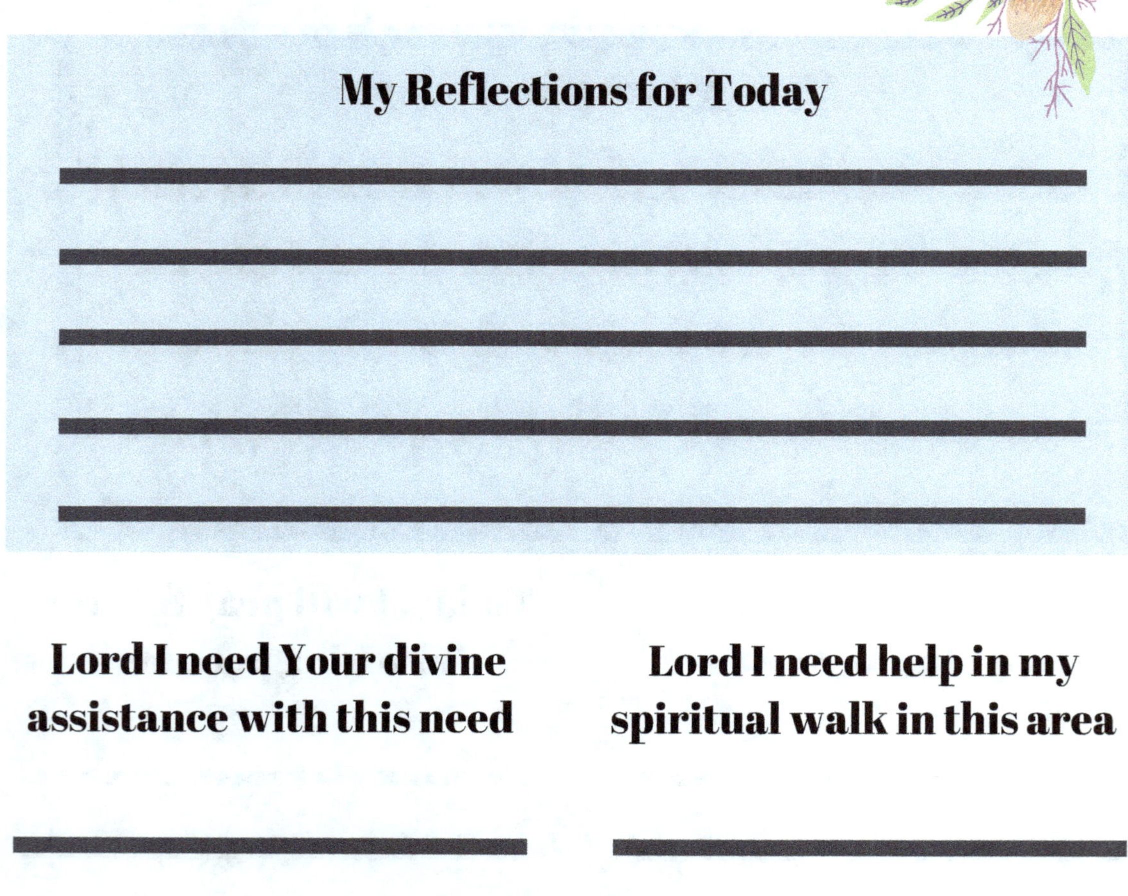

My Reflections for Today

Lord I need Your divine assistance with this need

Lord I need help in my spiritual walk in this area

"And rising very early in the morning, while it was still dark, he departed and went out to a desolate place, and there he prayed"
(Mark 1:35).

Paul's Fast

"And he was three days without sight, and neither did eat nor drink"   (Acts 9:9)

Date: _______________________________

My Key Verse for Today

____

____

____

____

Lord I thank You for

____

____

____

____

Today, I will pray for the following persons

____

____

____

____

My Reflections for Today

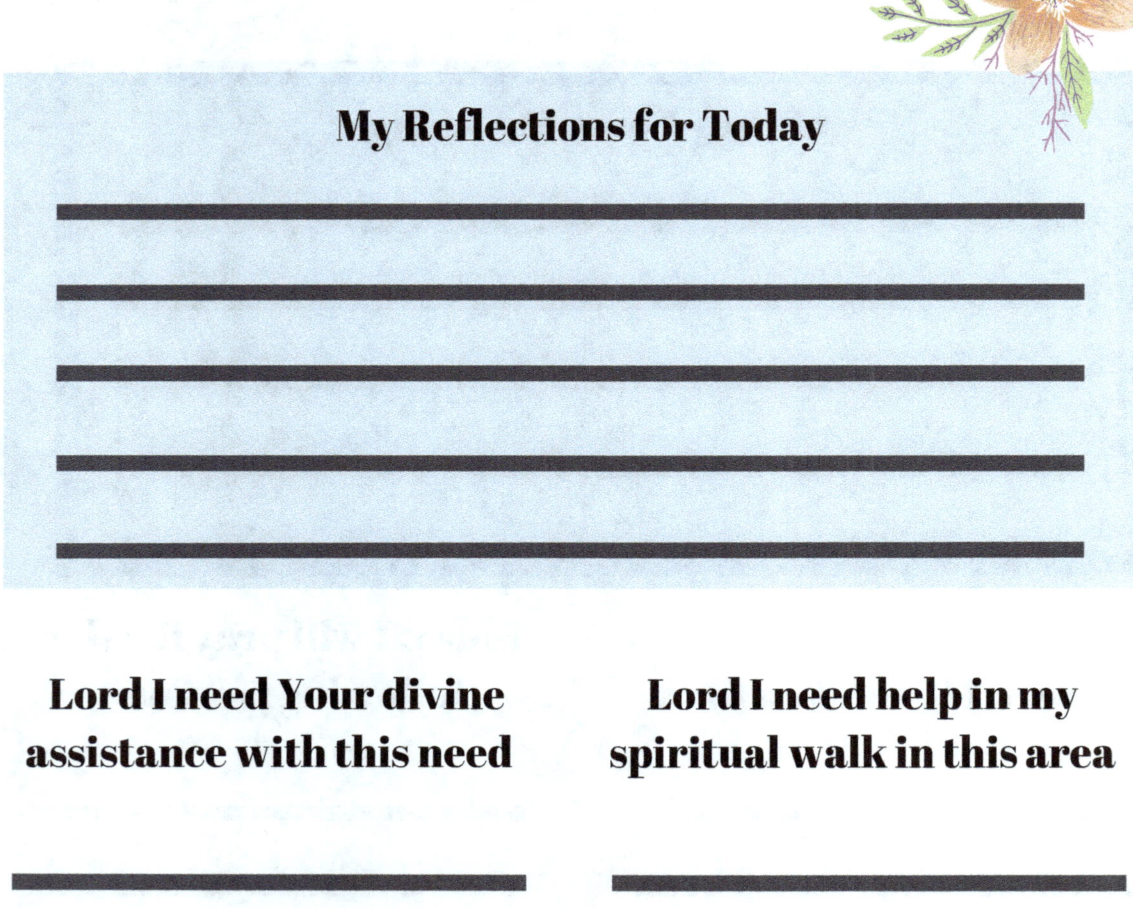

Lord I need Your divine assistance with this need

Lord I need help in my spiritual walk in this area

My Prayer

"And they devoted themselves to the apostles' teaching and the fellowship, to the breaking of bread and the prayers" (Acts 2:42)

Date: ______________________________

My Key Verse for Today

____

____

____

____

Lord I thank You for

____

____

____

____

____

____

Today, I will pray for the following persons

____

____

____

____

____

____

My Reflections for Today

Lord I need Your divine assistance with this need

Lord I need help in my spiritual walk in this area

"And without faith it is impossible to please him, for whoever would draw near to God must believe that he exists and that he rewards those who seek him" (Hebrews 11:6).

The Fast of John The Baptist

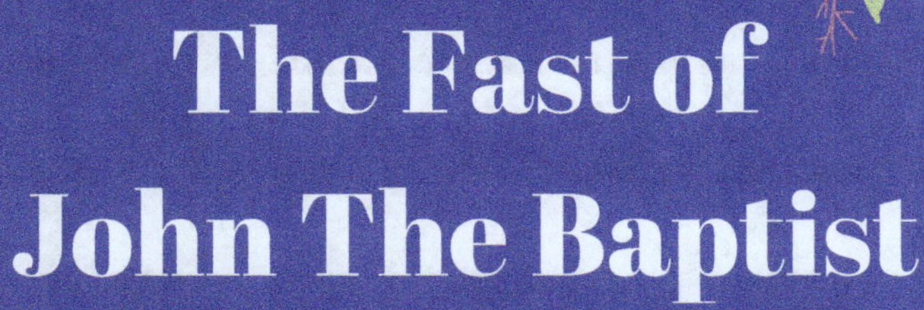

"For he shall be great in the sight of the Lord, and shall drink neither wine nor strong drink; and he shall be filled with the Holy Ghost, even from his mother's womb" (Luke 1:15)

Date: ___________________

My Key Verse for Today

____

____

____

____

Lord I thank You for

____

____

____

____

____

____

Today, I will pray for the following persons

____

____

____

____

____

____

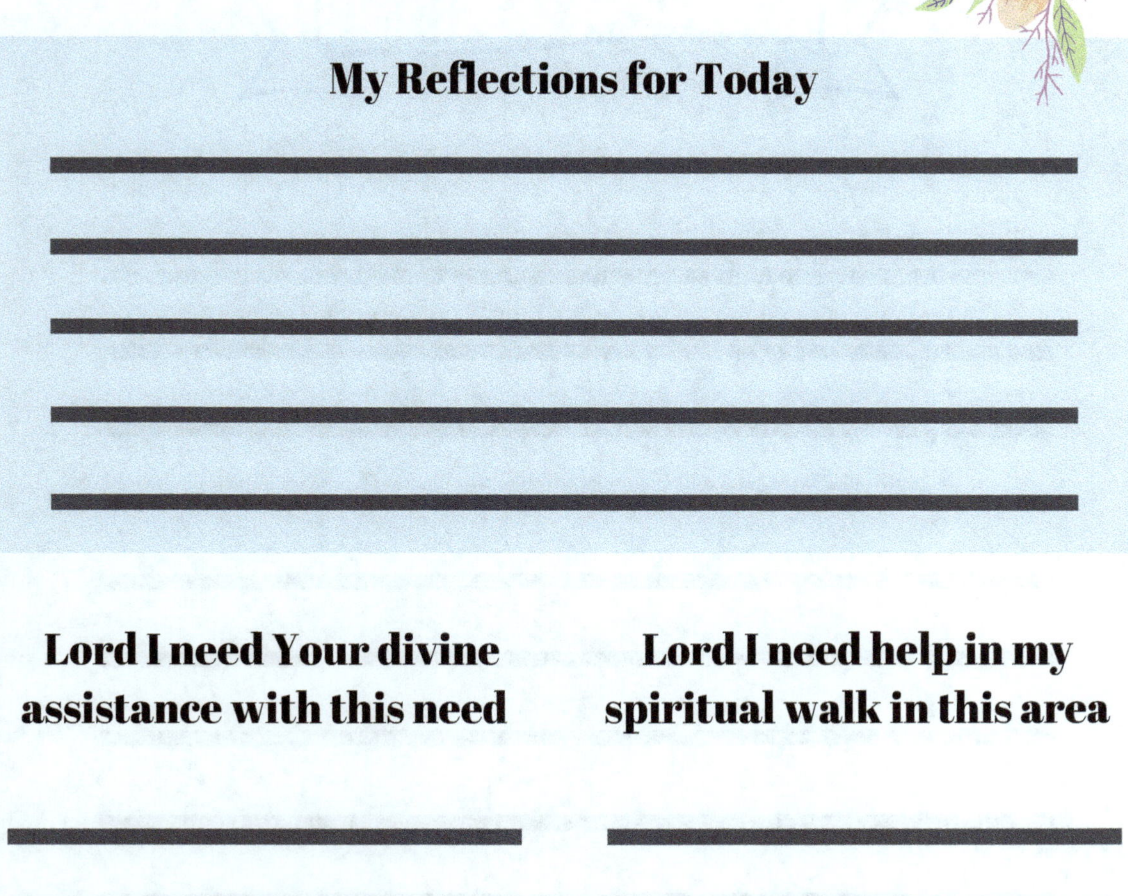

My Reflections for Today

Lord I need Your divine assistance with this need

Lord I need help in my spiritual walk in this area

____

____

____

____

____

____

____

____

____

____

"Likewise the Spirit helps us in our weakness. For we do not know what to pray for as we ought, but the Spirit himself intercedes for us with groanings too deep for words" (Romans 8:26).

Date: ______________________________

My Key Verse for Today

____

____

____

____

Lord I thank You for

____

____

____

____

____

____

Today, I will pray for the following persons

____

____

____

____

____

____

My Reflections for Today

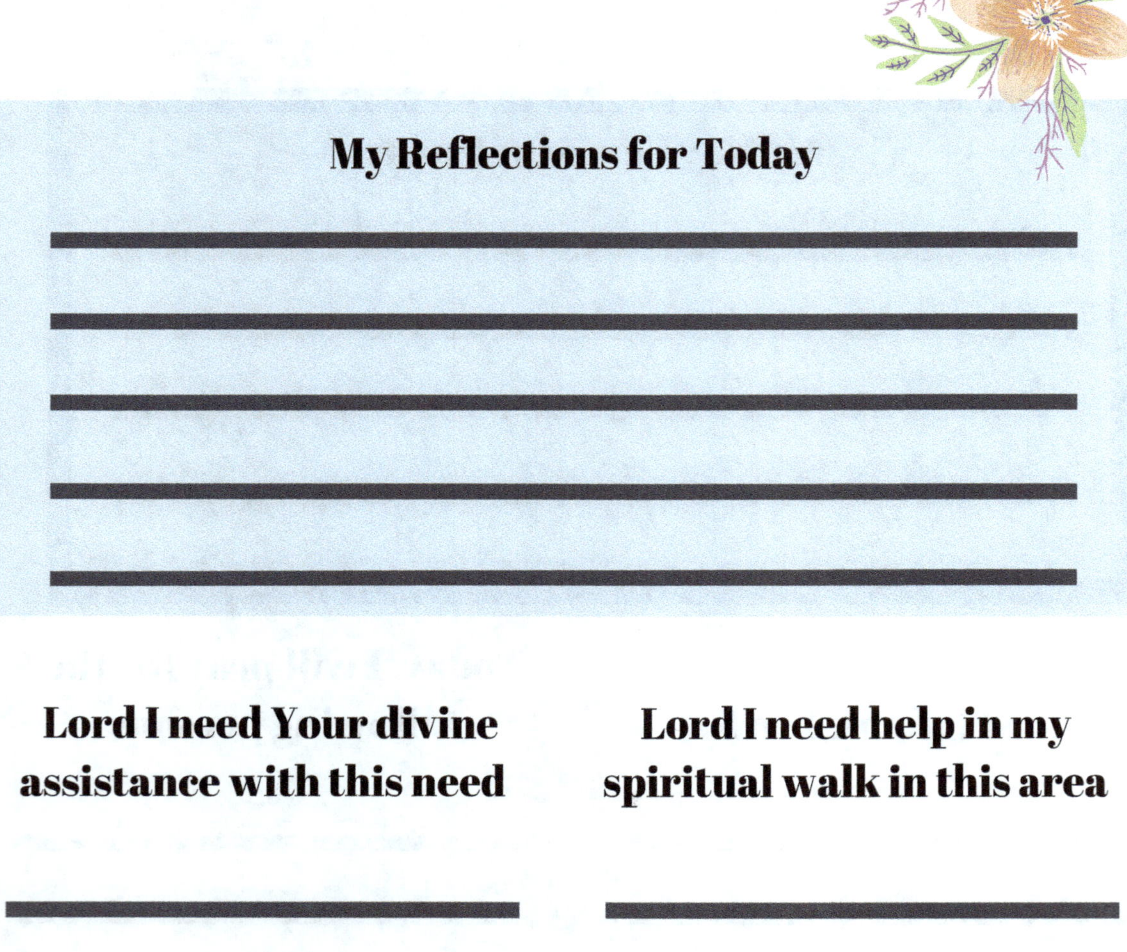

Lord I need Your divine assistance with this need

Lord I need help in my spiritual walk in this area

My Prayer

____

____

____

____

____

____

____

____

____

____

"If you abide in me, and my words abide in you, ask whatever you wish, and it will be done for you" (John 15:7).

Date: _______________________

My Key Verse for Today

____

____

____

____

Lord I thank You for

____

____

____

____

____

____

Today, I will pray for the following persons

____

____

____

____

____

____

My Reflections for Today

Lord I need Your divine assistance with this need

Lord I need help in my spiritual walk in this area

My Prayer

"I desire then that in every place the men should pray, lifting holy hands without anger or quarreling;" (1Tim. 2:8).

Daniel's Fast (10 Days)

"Prove thy servants, I beseech thee, ten days; and let them give us pulse to eat, and water to drink"
(Daniel 1:12)

Date: ______________________

My Key Verse for Today

Lord I thank You for

Today, I will pray for the following persons

My Reflections for Today

Lord I need Your divine assistance with this need

Lord I need help in my spiritual walk in this area

____

____

____

____

____

____

____

____

____

____

"If my people who are called by my name humble themselves, and pray and seek my face and turn from their wicked ways, then I will hear from heaven and will forgive their sin and heal their land" (2 Chronicles 7:14).

Date: _______________________________

My Key Verse for Today

____

____

____

____

Lord I thank You for

____

____

____

____

____

____

Today, I will pray for the following persons

____

____

____

____

____

____

My Reflections for Today

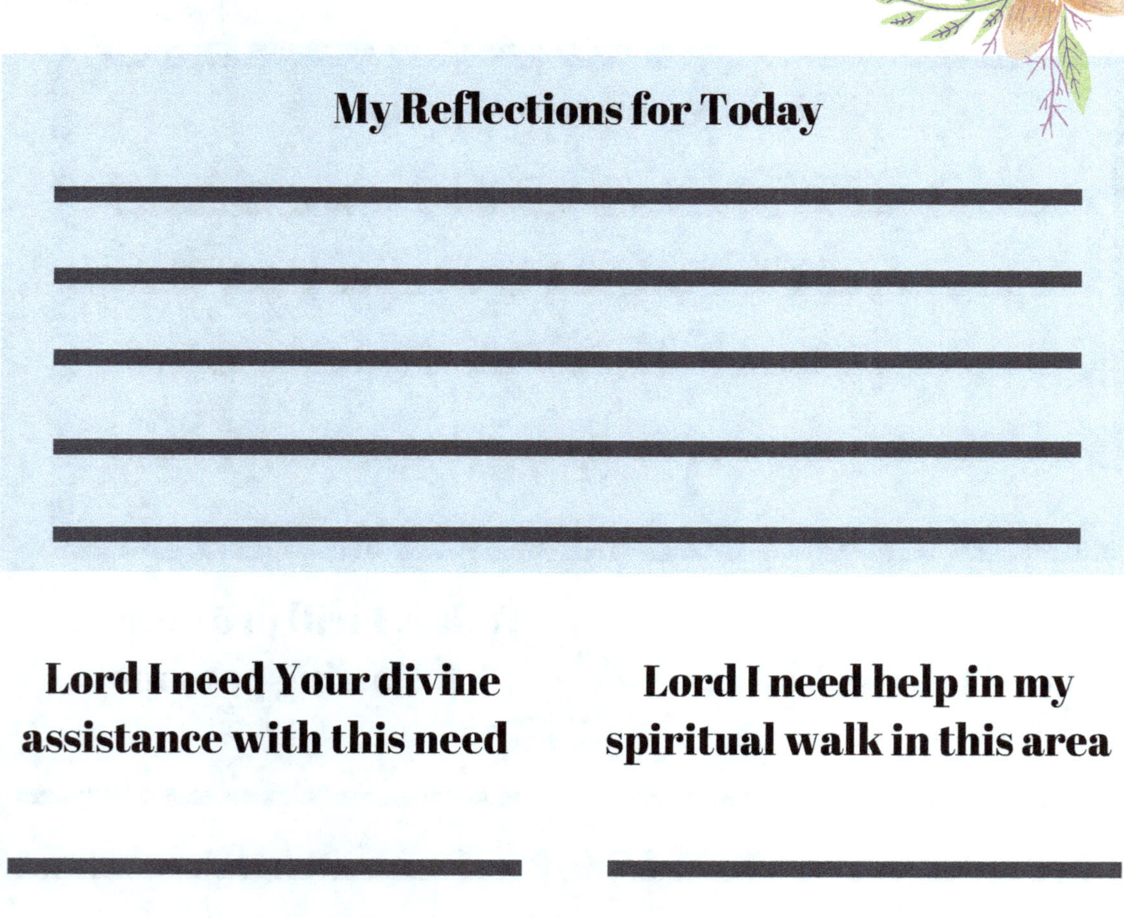

Lord I need Your divine assistance with this need

Lord I need help in my spiritual walk in this area

"Pray then like this: "Our Father in heaven, hallowed be your name. Your kingdom come, your will be done, on earth as it is in heaven. Give us this day our daily bread, and forgive us our debts, as we also have forgiven our debtors. And lead us not into temptation, but deliver us from evil" (Matthew 6:9-24).

Date: ______________________

My Key Verse for Today

____

____

____

____

Lord I thank You for

____

____

____

____

____

____

Today, I will pray for the following persons

____

____

____

____

____

____

My Reflections for Today

Lord I need Your divine assistance with this need

Lord I need help in my spiritual walk in this area

____

____

____

____

____

____

____

____

____

____

"In my distress I called upon the Lord, and cried unto my God: he heard my voice out of his temple, and my cry came before him, even into his ears" (Psalm 18:6).

The Disciples' Fast

"Howbeit this kind goeth not out but by prayer and fasting" (Matthew 17:21)

My Key Verse for Today

Lord I thank You for

Today, I will pray for the following persons

My Reflections for Today

Lord I need Your divine assistance with this need

Lord I need help in my spiritual walk in this area

____

____

____

____

____

____

____

____

____

____

"My voice shalt thou hear in the morning, O LORD; in the morning will I direct [my prayer] unto thee, and will look up (Pslam 5:3).

Date: _______________________

My Key Verse for Today

____

____

____

____

Lord I thank You for

____

____

____

____

____

____

Today, I will pray for the following persons

____

____

____

____

____

____

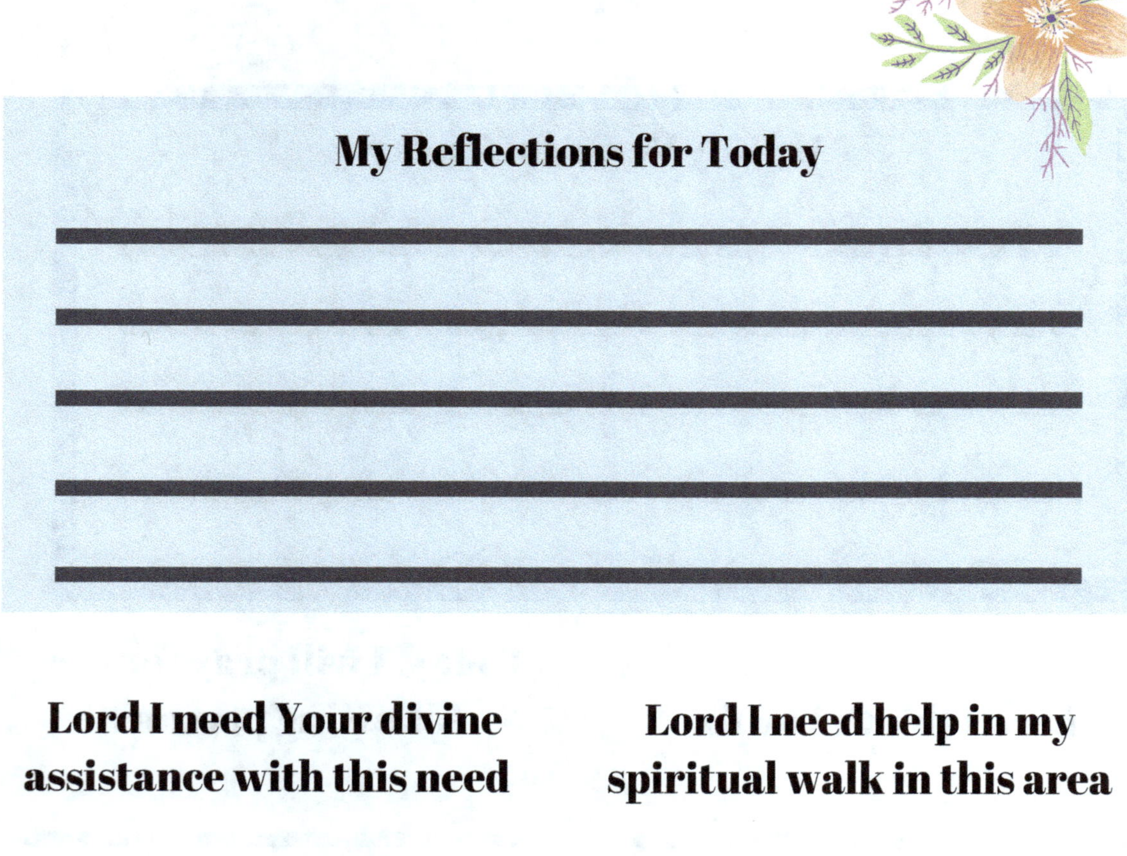

My Reflections for Today

Lord I need Your divine assistance with this need

Lord I need help in my spiritual walk in this area

My Prayer

____

____

____

____

____

____

____

____

____

____

"Watch and pray, that ye enter not into temptation: the spirit indeed is willing, but the flesh is weak" (Matthew 26:41).

Date: ______________________________

My Key Verse for Today

Lord I thank You for

Today, I will pray for the following persons

My Reflections for Today

Lord I need Your divine assistance with this need

Lord I need help in my spiritual walk in this area

"And whatsoever ye shall ask in my name, that will I do, that the Father may be glorified in the Son" (John 14:13).

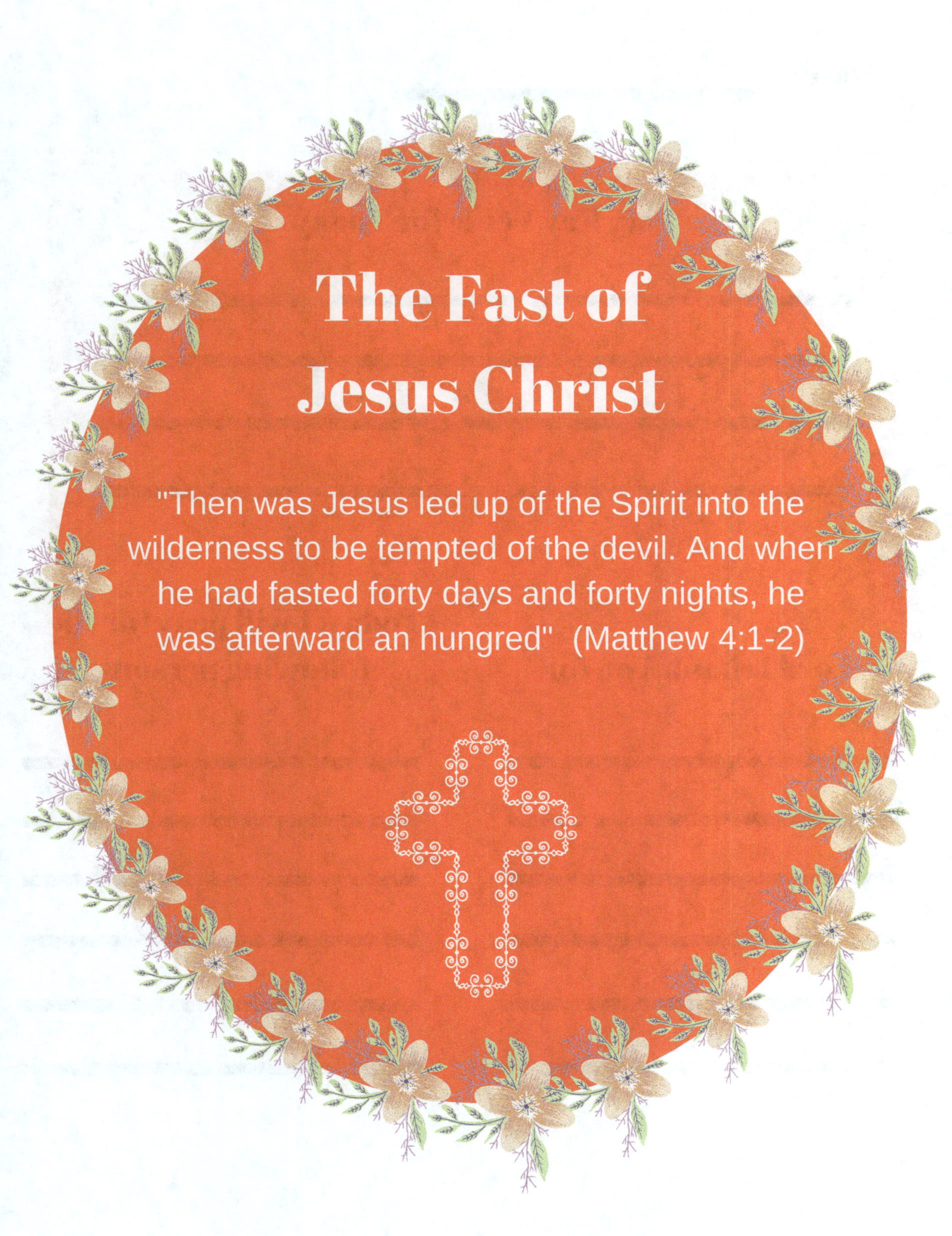

The Fast of
Jesus Christ

"Then was Jesus led up of the Spirit into the wilderness to be tempted of the devil. And when he had fasted forty days and forty nights, he was afterward an hungred" (Matthew 4:1-2)

Date: ___________________

My Key Verse for Today

____

____

____

____

Lord I thank You for

____

____

____

____

____

____

Today, I will pray for the following persons

____

____

____

____

____

____

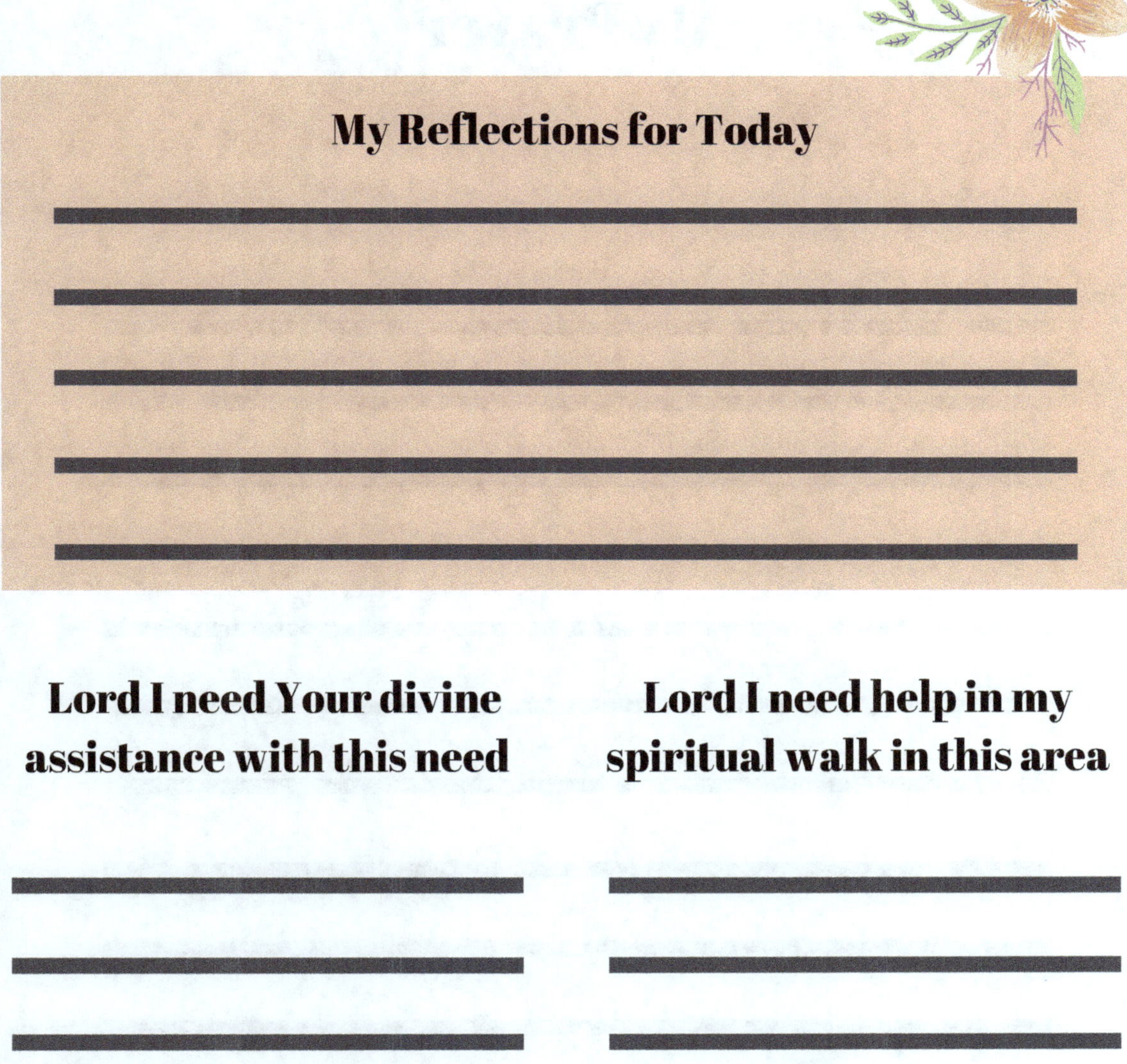

My Reflections for Today

Lord I need Your divine assistance with this need

Lord I need help in my spiritual walk in this area

____

____

____

____

____

____

____

____

____

____

"But thou, when thou prayest, enter into thy closet, and when thou hast shut thy door, pray to thy Father which is in secret; and thy Father which seeth in secret shall reward thee openly" (Matthew 6:6).

Answers to Prayers

"And at midnight Paul and Silas prayed, and sang praises unto God: and the prisoners heard them" (Acts 16:25).

Answers to Prayers

"Let us therefore come boldly unto the throne of grace, that we may obtain mercy, and find grace to help in time of need" (Hebrews 4:16).

Answers to Prayers

"Even now," declares the LORD, "return to me with all your heart, with fasting and weeping and mourning" (Joel 2:12).

Answers to Prayers

"For where two or three are gathered together in my name, there am I in the midst of them" (Matthew 18:20).

"But when ye pray, use not vain repetitions, as the heathen do: for they think that they shall be heard for their much speaking" (Matthew 6:7).

Answers to Prayers

"Call unto me, and I will answer thee, and show thee great and mighty things, which thou knowest not" (Jeremiah 33:3)

NOTES

"Therefore I say unto you, What things soever ye desire, when ye pray, believe that ye receive them, and ye shall have them" (Mark 11:24).

NOTES

"Continue in prayer, and watch in the same with thanksgiving"
(Colossians 4:2)

NOTES

NOTES

"Be careful for nothing; but in every thing by prayer and supplication with thanksgiving let your requests be made known unto God. And the peace of God, which passeth all understanding, shall keep your hearts and minds through Christ Jesus" (Philippians 4:6-7).

NOTES

Rejoice evermore. Pray without ceasing. In every thing give thanks: for this is the will of God in Christ Jesus concerning you" (1Thess. 5:16-18).

NOTES

"For verily I say unto you, That whosoever shall say unto this mountain, Be thou removed, and be thou cast into the sea; and shall not doubt in his heart, but shall believe that those things which he saith shall come to pass; he shall have whatsoever he saith"
(Mark 11:23-25).

PRE FAST
GROCERY LIST

PRE FAST
GROCERY LIST

PRE FAST
GROCERY LIST

About the Author

Andrea Clarke Pratt retired in 2018 after more than 30 years in the corporate world. She then pursued the field of Education and is currently teaching at a High School. Her hunger for the Word of God led her to complete a Master's Degree in Theology.

Andrea is also the Author of the book ***"I'm Loving My Age: A Believer's Guide to Aging Gracefully and Words of Hope for the Elderly"***. The book is a compilation of promises from the Bible, poems on aging, legacy statements, and even a family tree that encourages its older readers to celebrate all the wisdom and insight they have acquired over the years and help them realize that age is not something to be looked down upon. The older generation can still be used by God to awaken everyone, including the younger generation, to what it means to know and love Jesus.

Contact:

P. O. Box N-8579
Colony Village
Nassau, New Providence
The Bahamas
adpratt6@gmail.com